SWING around the SUN

poems by

Barbara Juster Esbensen

art by

Cheng-Khee Chee (spring)

Janice Lee Porter (summer)

Mary GrandPré (fall)

Stephen Gammell (winter)

SWING around the SUN

Carolrhoda Books, Inc./Minneapolis

Spring

art by **Cheng-Khee Chee**

Seascape

Like an echo
For the eye,
The mountain reaches blue
From a bright, exploding sea.
Snow crown
And breaker
Dazzle the wind,
And a gull hangs
Like an icy flake
Between.

March

Wind swooping
And howling,
Blustering, yowling,
Caught in the branches
Of skeleton trees;

Rain dripping
On bumbershoots,
Splashing on rubber boots,
Filling the sidewalks
With miniature seas.

Umbrellas turned
Inside-out,
Hats blowing all about,
Clouds flying swiftly
In Heaven's gray arch;

Crocuses pink as spice,
Mud puddles,
Melting ice;
Lambs frisking,
Kites flying,
Now it is March!

Umbrellas

Umbrellas bloom
Along our street
Like flowers on a stem.
And almost everyone
I meet
Is holding one of them.

Under my umbrella-top,
Splashing through the town,
I wonder why the tulips
Hold umbrellas
Up-side-down!

The Return

Bound with silence,
Chained with ice,
Frozen, muffled, deep,
The world begins
To move again,
Stirring from its sleep.

The tip-tap-tup
Of icicles
Awakes the melting night.
And from the sky
A wedge of cry:
Returning geese in flight.

Robin

Does he hear the grass grow,
Seeds split wide?
Whatever does he listen to,
Head-tipped-side?

When he hops and listens,
And cocks a watching eye,
Does he hear the spring come?
Or dinner scooting by?

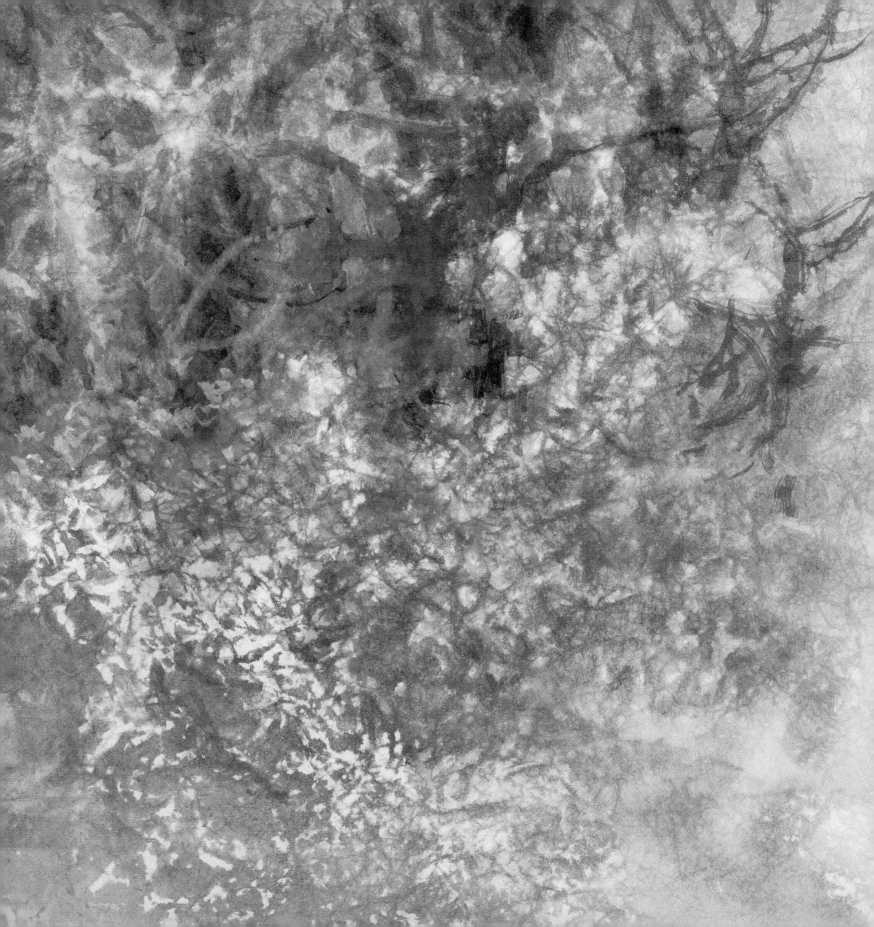

Summer

art by Janice Lee Porter

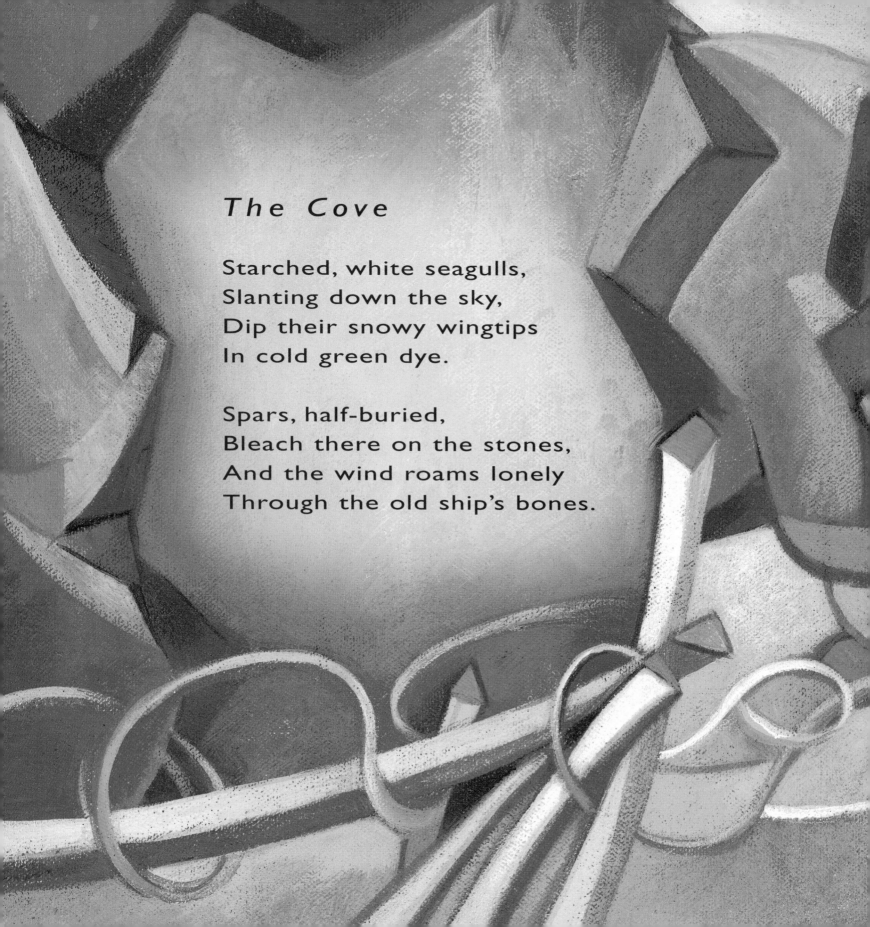

The Cove

Starched, white seagulls,
Slanting down the sky,
Dip their snowy wingtips
In cold green dye.

Spars, half-buried,
Bleach there on the stones,
And the wind roams lonely
Through the old ship's bones.

Vacant Lot

Nobody comes here,
Nobody mows
The hip-high grass
Where the green snake goes.

Nobody bothers
The tumbling bee,
The flax-flowers
Blue as a slice of sea.

Forgotten by everybody,
Silent in the sun,
Dragonflies shimmer there,
Lizards run.

Yellow

Yellow sun
And yellow sky,
A dandelion's
Yellow eye;

Yellow pollen
Dusts the breeze,
And yellow
Lights the summer trees.

A yellow buzzing
Prints the air;
In dappled yellow
Dreams the pear.

And from the finch's
Yellow throat
One golden, flowing
Yellow note!

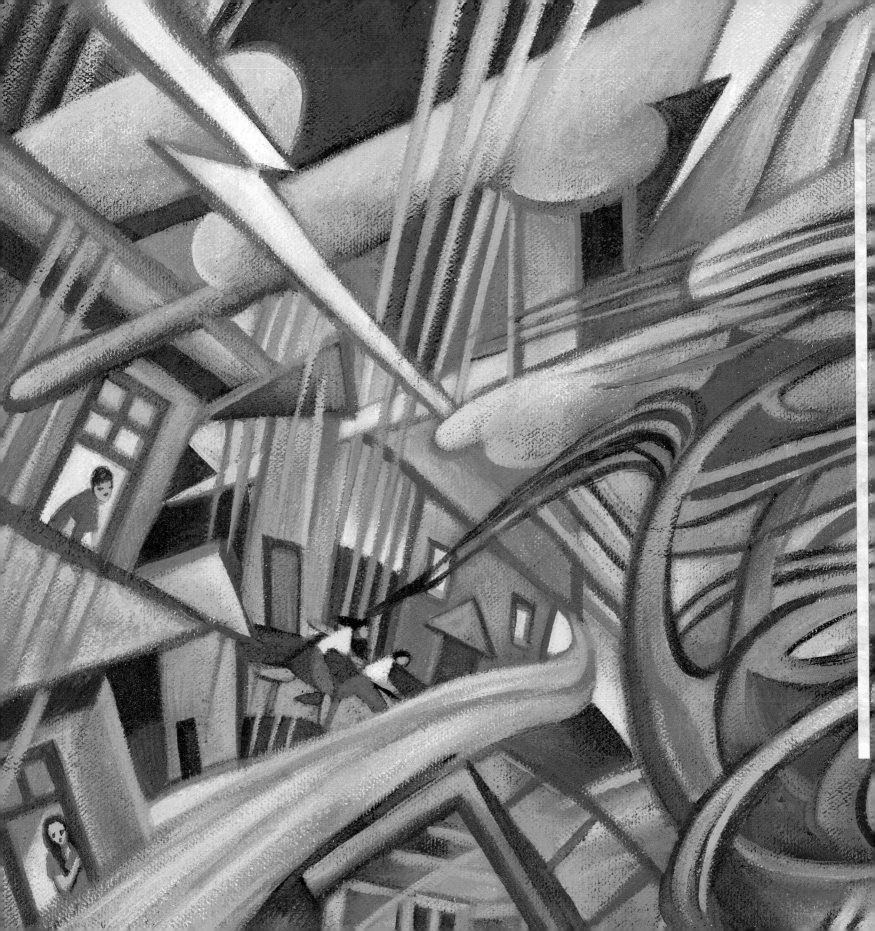

Storm

Day is night!
The world is black;
The thunder snaps
With a splitting crack!

Beaks of lightning
Rip the air
And willows swing
Their streaming hair.

Threads of rain
Bind earth to sky;
The gutter's torrent
Rushes by.

No house has shape,
No tree a form;
The town is lost
In summer storm!

Fireworks

The sky's a fiery garden
That scatters in the breeze,
Vying with the fireflies
Glowing in the trees.

Spangling the darkness,
Velvety and deep,
The last exploding starfall
Crumbles into sleep.

Fall

art by **Mary GrandPré**

October Alchemy

Empty garden,
Withered flower,
Elm leaves fall
In a golden shower.

Wind runs howling,
Rain slants cold;
Elm leaves pave
The streets with gold.

Discovery

Within its polished universe
The apple holds a star,
A secret constellation
To scatter near and far.

Let a knife discover
Where the five points hide;
Split the shining ruby
And find the star inside!

Autumn Concert

Together,
In the sapphire sky
They float:
The milkweed
And a burnished
Trumpet note.

Hallowe'en

Leaf piles smoke in the whispering dark,
Goblins prowl the streets;
Silent witches haunt the park,
Ghosts unfurl their sheets.

Noiseless footfall on the stair,
Thumping in the hall;
Someone knows just who to scare—
And *I* scare best of all!

Prediction

Yesterday,
It was not there,
This pointed flavor
In the air.

Yesterday,
We gathered leaves
To wear like emblems
On our sleeves.

But now there is
A different feel:
The silver sky
Has rims of steel.

And in the night,
(I know! I know!)
The snow will fly!
The snow! The snow!

Winter

art by **Stephen Gammell**

First Snow

Snow stars fall
On faces and hats;
They twinkle the ears
And the fur of our cats.

They fall and they spin
In the cold, black night—
Pointed and sparkling,
White! White! White!

Snow Clown

Let's roll him uphill!
Let's roll him down!
Now pile him all together,
A fat Snow Clown!

Twigs and coal and branches
For arms and legs and smile;
A Snow Clown's in our garden
For just a snowy while!

Skating

We glitter and fly
Beneath the sky
And lean against the gale.

Our feet wear blades
Of diamond dust;
We etch a frosty trail.

The brittle pond
Is ringed with snow,
The pines are brushed with black.

Around we skim,
Around the rim,
Around the rim, and back.

The Wind Woman

The Wind's white fingers
Are thin and sharp,
And she plays all night
On an icy harp.

On her icy harp
Of stiff, black trees,
She plays her songs,
And the rivers freeze.

Snowfall

Who shook the night
And made the feathers
Fly?
They fall and lift and fall
Without a sound.

And as I stand
Beneath the street lamp,
I can scarcely tell
The rooftop from the ground.

Who tipped the night?
Who let the feathers whirl?
They circle softly
Round and round this place,

And blur the footsteps
Of a little girl,
And frost her hair
And melt upon her face.

About the Artists

World renowned watercolorist **Cheng-Khee Chee's** paintings have been widely exhibited throughout the United States and have earned him over one hundred national awards. In 1991 he illustrated the children's bestseller, *Old Turtle*. He lives in Duluth, Minnesota, where he is an Associate Professor of Art Emeritus at the University of Minnesota.

Janice Lee Porter has illustrated a number of award-winning children's books, including *Hope* and *Aunt Clara Brown*, a *School Library Journal* Best Book and ABA *Bookselling This Week* Kids' Pick of the Lists. She lives in Minneapolis, Minnesota.

Mary GrandPré has illustrated several children's books, including *Chin Yu Min and the Ginger Cat*, *Bat Wings and the Curtain of Night*, and the American editions of J. K. Rowling's popular Harry Potter series. She has received awards for her work from The Society of Illustrators, Communications Arts, and others. She lives in Saint Paul, Minnesota.

Stephen Gammell, a friend of Barbara Juster Esbensen, has illustrated more than fifty children's books, including *The Burger and the Hot Dog,* a collection of children's poetry. He has received numerous awards for his work and was honored with a Caldecott Medal for *Song and Dance Man*. He lives in Saint Paul, Minnesota.

Barbara Juster Esbensen
1925-1996

Raised in Madison, Wisconsin, Barbara developed the courage to play with words from the books of L. M. Montgomery. In 1939 she showed her favorite teacher, Miss Eulalie Beffel, one of her poems. Ms. Beffel's encouragement changed Barbara's life. She said, "You are a writer."

Although always interested in writing, Barbara chose to pursue her bachelor's degree in art education at the University of Wisconsin. For many years, she taught art to grades K-12 and was a creative arts consultant at the College of Saint Scholastica in Duluth, Minnesota.

Barbara published her first book, *Swing around the Sun*, in 1965 with Lerner Publications. After taking a break to raise six children, Barbara continued writing. A complete list of Barbara's books is available on the Barbara Juster Esbensen memorial website at <www.ttinet.com/bje>.

In 1994 Barbara was honored with the National Council of Teachers of English (NCTE) Award for Excellence in Poetry for Children for her aggregate body of work. Barbara's books won a number of awards, including the Minnesota Book Award for *The Star Maiden*, an NCTE Teacher's Choice Award for *Great Northern Diver: The Loon*, a National Science Teacher's Associate Notable Children's book Award for *Tiger with Wings: The Great Horned Owl*, and the Lee Bennett Hopkins Award for *Dance with Me*. In 2002 she was posthumously awarded the Kerlan Award "in recognition of singular attainments in the creation of children's literature."

An active supporter of the arts, Barbara enjoyed visiting schools and teaching children about the beauty and creativity of words. A teaching award has been established in memory of Barbara. The award is given each year to the teacher who has made the best use of her book *A Celebration of Bees: Helping Children Write Poetry*.

Note from the Publisher

Early in 1964, just five years after founding Lerner Publications, Harry Lerner was visited by Barbara Fumagalli. The art professor wielded her sketches for a children's poetry collection and brought along her friend Barbara Juster Esbensen, who had written the accompanying poems. Harry thought both the artwork and the poems had kid and teacher appeal. He published *Swing around the Sun* the following year. The whole book was an elegant display of 1960's design—the original cover sported an orange and yellow starburst wrapped around the black title type. The interior artwork was all done in black line illustration. *Swing around the Sun* went on to sell out of four printings.

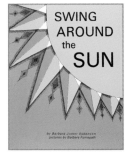

Barbara Juster Esbensen spent the next nineteen years raising six children with her husband, Tory. When she returned to writing, however, she did so with renewed vigor. Resuming with *Cold Stars and Fireflies* (Crowell, 1984), she published seventeen books of poetry and nonfiction for children between 1984 and 1997. Notably, Barbara only returned to the rhyming style of her first book when she wrote *Dance with Me* (HarperCollins, 1995). To her surprise, it turned out to be one of her most successful titles, receiving the Lee Bennett Hopkins Award for Excellence in Children's Poetry. Her last book, *The Night Rainbow* (Orchard, 2000), was published posthumously.

The appeal of Barbara's verse in *Swing around the Sun* has endured many years. In remaking this collection, we reduced the number of poems per season from seven to five. The poems in this collection continue to resonate as strongly as they did in 1965. With breathtaking new illustrations from some of the finest contemporary artists, we are pleased to present these poems to a whole new generation of readers.

Enjoy!

Adam Lerner
President & Publisher
Carolrhoda Books

For
my mother and father
and for
Eulalie C. Beffel
who said,
"There are words . . . "
—Barbara Juster Esbensen, 1965

Carolrhoda Books, Inc.
A division of Lerner Publishing Group
241 First Avenue North
Minneapolis, MN 55401 U.S.A.

Website address: www.lernerbooks.com

Library of Congress Cataloging-in-Publication Data

Esbensen, Barbara Juster.
     Swing around the sun / by Barbara Juster Esbensen ; illustrated by
Cheng-Khee Chee . . . [et al.].
        p.   cm.
     Summary: A collection of poems that celebrates the seasons, with
illustrations for each season by a different Minnesota artist.
     ISBN: 0–87614–143–2 (lib. bdg. : alk. paper)
     1. Seasons—Juvenile poetry. 2. Children's poetry, American.
[1. Seasons—Poetry. 2. American poetry.] I. Chee, Cheng-Khee, ill.
II. Title.
PS3555.S24 S94 2003
811'.54—dc21   2002007980

Manufactured in the United States of America
1 2 3 4 5 6 – JR – 08 07 06 05 04 03